Glimpses of Light

by Susan Grace Gordon

Published by Joshua Gordon BookWorks.
joshuagordonbookworks.com

Copyright © Susan Gordon 2015

All rights reserved. Reproduction and distribution are forbidden.
No part of this publication shall be reproduced, stored in a retrieval system, or transmitted by any other means, electronic, mechanical, photocopying, recording, or otherwise, without prior written permission from the author.

ISBN 978-0-9940592-2-2

ENDORSEMENTS

Sue's insight and attitude about life have lifted me to a higher place as a human being. As you read the pages of this book, you will be enlightened, encouraged, and empowered by the words from this woman's heart. In struggle, she found strength. In the face of difficulty, she found peace, and in the most difficult of circumstances, she found hope that comes from God alone. As you read these pages, you will come to know Sue, and our prayer is that you will find the very same hope she has found. That hope is in Christ Himself.
- Pastor Daniel Ishee, Zephryhills, Florida

"The theme of Sue's poems is the fruit of her daily walk with her Heavenly Father. The message of Sue's poems is the fruit of her daily reading of the Word of God. Through the reading of her poems we are spiritually blessed and inspired and drawn closer to the One who loved us and gave Himself for us, even Jesus Christ our Lord.
- Rev. John W. Roberts
'Pastored in Ontario and Quebec 1947 – 2008'

This book is dedicated with love to:
God,
my husband Dave,
my children and step-children:
Cindy, Donna and Dan, Lori-Anne, and Mike,
their spouses,
and all my grandchildren.

Introduction

For many years I wondered why I was on earth; what was the reason for my life; what was the purpose of it all and where did I fit into the scheme of things. I believed that God and Jesus and satan were real, and the Bible was God's book of instruction to the world. But the 2000 years between Jesus' life on earth and mine made the connection a problem. I just didn't get it!
Did I personally have a purpose? Did God actually know me? I had to find out.

So my quest for truth and peace began.

These poems and stories were written over many years during my search for and my walk with the Lord. I have been greatly blessed and you can be too no matter where or who you are or what has happened in your past.

-Susan Grace Gordon

Table of Contents

Introduction vii

About Sue

    Who Am I?................... 3

    Sue's Search for the Lord...................... 4

Nature

    The Truest Fish Story..................... 11

    Before You Go................................ 14

    The Cracked Rock........................... 15

    A Labour of Love.............................. 16

    Sitting in a Bog................................ 18

    The Piercing Truth........................... 20

    Look Up... 23

    In Search of the Great Blue Heron........ 24

    Snail Tale....................................... 25

    Loud Whisperings............................ 27

Joy and Thankfulness

    Appreciation..................................... 33

    Cancer Scare.................................... 34

	My Daily Prayer.............................	36
	Peace	37
	Pathways.....................................	38
Faith		
	The Beginning...............................	41
	A Purpose in Life...........................	42
	Be Prepared..................................	43
	The Balloon...................................	44
	The Ladder Bookmark....................	45
	The Answer...................................	46
	The Knot for Life...........................	47
Spiritual Warfare		
	The Armour of God........................	51
	A Choice to Make..........................	53
Helping Others		
	Ultimate Power..............................	57
	First Things First	61
	Through the Ages	64
	Small Steps Forward......................	65

The Awesome Power of Prayer............	68
Nudges...	69
Choking Ordeal.................................	70
The Ripple Effect..............................	73
Valuable Service...............................	74
Point of View....................................	76
Baby Shoes.......................................	77
Your Memory of Me..........................	78
How to Shine Your Light for Others	79

Salvation

Wonderful News...............................	83
The Anchor.......................................	84
The Change Within...........................	85
The Door of Life...............................	86
God is Real.......................................	87
Eulogy Comfort.................................	89
Transformation.................................	90

Considering Salvation

Reflection...	97

	Destination…………………………..	98
	Too Late……………………………………….	99
	The Verdict…………………………..	102
	Life's Shelter……………………….…	103
	Premature……………………………….…	104
Change		
	On Being Brave…………………….	107
	How in the World I Ever Quit Smoking…	110
	The Stash……………………………..	114
Christian Life		
	The Christian Farmer – An Ode to My Dad……………………………….…	119
	An Ode to My Mom – Margaret Grace Alton……………………………..	120
	Criticism……………………………….…	121
	Daybreak………………………………..	122
	Last Chance ………………………..	123
	Truth………………………………..	124
	Remember……………………………….	125
	Repose………………………………….	126
	Through the Fog…………………….	128

My White-Haired Soul Sister................	129
My Daily Boost.................................	132
Our Worth..	133
We Are Never Alone.........................	134
Whisper a Little Louder Lord................	135

About Sue

Who Am I?

I was born on a farm and country is my life,
I've been someone's daughter, mother, sister and a wife.
My feet are in the garden, in a flowerbed or bush,
My hands do many crafts and a pen I like to push.
I sing bass with the men for my voice is very low,
When I hear people's troubles both my eyes may overflow.
Though I've lived half a century now God is in my heart,
In spite of all my past mistakes, I have a brand new start.

God's given me a gift to write my feelings with a pen,
In poetry and story form for women and for men.
For there was space within my heart - a place I couldn't fill,
Until I turned to God above and gave Him my free will.
We each have great potential through the gifts the Lord did give.

So we can be of use to God wherever we may live.
I want to say that there is hope, no matter what your strife,
For Jesus wants to fill your heart with peace throughout your life.

Sue's Search for the Lord

I spent the years from birth until my twenties attending a different Church than the fellowship I now attend. I was baptized as an infant by the minister sprinkling a few drops of water on my head. It was also called being Christened and accepted by the congregation into the body of the Church.

I went to Sunday school every Sunday throughout my childhood and remember hearing the children's stories and colouring pictures of Jesus in colouring books. Upon reaching the age of twelve, the children—including me—took catechism classes and joined the Church as a member, now being allowed to partake in Communion.

Most teenagers found that particular Church out of touch in the lives of that age group with little in the service pertaining to them, so the youth took no part except to sing in the choir if they chose.

Most teenagers—including me—quit going to Church as soon as they could find an excuse not to attend. There didn't seem to be anything there for us.

What was my mindset? I was a baptized Christian and would go to heaven when I died. A personal relationship with Jesus never entered my mind as no one actually talked openly about Jesus.

I felt Church participation was for old people, and except for special occasions, my life carried on without it. During the next twenty-five years I got married and had three wonderful children who were also baptized in that same Church. We moved away and after sixteen years we divorced. It was a spiteful, bitter divorce.

During these years life didn't turn out the way I had planned. People didn't do what I had hoped. My dreams for a sunny, happy future were a sad, unhappy myth and people I had trusted weren't trustworthy.

I became depressed and filled with hate for past events. From the stress of trying to cope alone, I was exhausted and a real mess. It was getting harder and harder to put up a happy, but artificial front for anyone. I had always tried to be a good wife, a good mother and person in the community. But felt there was something crucial missing in my life and that it had to do with God.

I knew a very few people that I considered to be "true Christians". These people had overcome hardships, were more in-depth in their religion and truly seemed to have a personal relationship with God. They had an aura of peace and confidence, a look that radiated tranquility and security. That's what I wanted—to become a true Christian—but didn't know how.

After months of frustration, I came to the conclusion that I just had to talk to one of these real people and I knew one—my doctor who was also my friend. I went to him and asked for help. He had that quality I wanted and needed desperately. It was peace. My doctor counselled me for two years and I fought him every step of the way because of my stubborn determination to be self-reliant. But I kept coming back and he never gave up on me. I would ask him a question and then disagree with his answer. He made me angry, but he made me think and I started to see my life from other perspectives. I tell you—Christians just don't give up on anyone—ever.

I had to take responsibility for my actions and learn how to forgive before I could be forgiven.

During these years, I went to a different denomination Church alone a few times and always left in tears feeling as if I didn't belong there with those happy people. One day on the way home, I stopped the car in an isolated spot called Proudfoot Swamp, and asked Jesus to come into my life. I sat there in the car and felt peace flowing into my heart and filling it completely, and I knew the Lord had truly come into my life. It was an amazing experience. But I continued trying to keep control of my life and nothing seemed to change. I was really discouraged.

I went to the Bible bookstore on the pretence of buying a book for someone else—not wanting anyone to know that I needed it myself. I was afraid that someone might ask me a question and I couldn't answer—horrors— and I was near forty already. I bought two books for my mother but also read them myself. My doctor said that if a Christian book caught my eye, there would be something in it that was necessary for me to learn and it would be a way God was guiding me.

My hunger for knowledge about God and Jesus grew and I read more books, and in each one I found a little piece of hope. Finally I bought and read the true autobiography of Crying Wind, and realized that Jesus was already in my heart and showed me what peace was like on that day in Proudfoot Swamp, but I hadn't turned over my "will" to Him or asked God to take over my life, and that I would do what He wanted—not what I wanted.

That was the key—control. I hadn't given God a chance. I asked the Lord to come into my heart when I was twelve and He did, and for all those years I ignored Him and did everything my own way. I asked him to help me do things my way, and it didn't work. I asked God to change people I couldn't change myself—nothing happened.

When I understood and totally surrendered myself to Jesus—not my will but Thy will be done, I found real peace, forgiveness and joy. He'd been there all along—just waiting for me.
God gave each of us total free will, the ability to make our own decisions at all times. I already know the outcome when I don't ask the Lord for guidance and plunge ahead on my own.

> *Ask, and it will be given to you;*
> *seek, and you will find;*
> *knock, and it will be opened to you.*
> *(Matthew 7:7 NKJV)*

Nature

The Truest Fish Story

There are carp in our lake. Big fish. My book says some carp can reach forty inches in length, but we've only seen them about one-third of that size. Most of the carp here are about fourteen to eighteen inches long.

Every spring, the carp swim along the shoreline. Probably breeding, they roil in very shallow water, creating a noisy commotion of splashing turmoil throughout the day and night. It's an amazing sight to watch all these big fish swimming so close to shore but they never seem to get stranded on land even when half their backs are sometimes out of the water.

Carp swim side by side in groups and you may see ten fish at one time. If one gets too far out of the water or wants to turn, the splashing and roiling begins until they get straightened out again. Carp slowly cruise around and look very easy to catch. Wrong! If you walk toward the water, they're gone in an instant, into the deep where you can't see them.

A few years ago I decided to try and catch one with a net. Just to have a good look at it and be able to say I'd caught a carp with a net. I couldn't reach any from shore; they stayed a little too far out if I stood at the water's edge. I took a few swipes with the net - not even close!

The next brilliant idea was for me to stand IN THE WATER and trap them between myself and shore. Sounded simple! Off came the shoes and socks, and I waded up to my knees into the frigid Canadian lake water. There I stood, absolutely still and also freezing, waiting for the stupid fish to forget I was there and swim back to within reach. I waited and waited! And waited! Finally the carp began swimming closer and closer until once again they were beside me. I felt like a great blue heron ready to strike.

The instant I tensed up and moved the net they were gone. So I would shift my position to be more ready, and wait - again. Here they would come closer and closer—twelve feet, ten feet, eight feet, six feet, six feet, six feet, five feet, three feet, six feet, one foot—too fast, three feet, two feet. I'd plunge the net and they'd disappear into the depths before the net hit the water. After many fruitless attempts and when my legs and feet were completely numb from the ice cold water, I dejectedly waded back to shore, hoping the neighbours hadn't been watching the performance.

Yesterday my ninety-one year old father came up and sure enough the carp were roiling. He was amazed. Dad stood at the very edge of the lake and the carp churned in the water right at his feet for minutes at a time.

So I walked to the shed and got the net.

This time however I was smarter. I stood poised to strike with lightning speed at the edge of our property line, the stone-pile wall built in a line from on-shore out into the water. There the fish would be swimming along and come to a halt at this stone obstacle. They would roil around a few seconds longer before finding their way around the underwater mound of stones.

Dad went to the cottage and carried down a lawn chair to sit and watch me.

I positioned myself at the waterline and all the fish disappeared. But I could hear them splashing directly behind the cedar shrub I was standing beside. About four feet away where I couldn't reach them. Stupid fish! I waited. And waited!

Finally the carp started to swim closer but not near enough. I was poised for action and bent a little forward with my arms raised and holding the net in the air. My back was aching. My feet were getting cold. Dad was getting bored.

Oh! Three fish were swimming right toward me. I lunged. Stepped into the water with my shoes on. Hit one fish on the back with the net but missed it. And they were gone.

Okay, next try. I changed my stance a little to get better balance. Dad got up and went around the side of the cottage - probably to laugh. I waited and thought again of the great blue heron.

After another half hour with aching back, freezing feet and feeling very frustrated, I put down the net and started another project. Immediately a group of carp reappeared and roiled for minutes in exactly the same spot I had been standing. My dear old father, bless his heart, didn't laugh in front of me. He did say that the fish could see us much better than we could see them. Soothing words for a bruised ego I must say. Wish you'd been there.

Before You Go

Take time to smell a flower;
Touch a mushroom;
Feel a feather;
Watch an inch worm;
Feel the breeze upon your face;
Smell cut grass;
Lay in leaves;
Watch a tree sway in the wind;
Find the big dipper in the night sky;
Step in a mud puddle in your bare feet;
Write on birch bark;
Look at a full moon;
Pat a cow;
Taste rhubarb;
They are God's gifts to us.
Don't miss it.

The Cracked Rock

I recently went for a walk along a lakeshore covered with large rocks and small stones. Picking my way through the barren rubble, I noticed something green on top of one stone about the size of my hand. There was a little plant growing on the top. I picked the stone up and noticed the smallest crack where the plants' roots had grown within the rock. With continual nourishment of sunlight and rain, this tiny plant would grow larger, its roots become stronger and eventually fill the crack with such pressure that it would break the rock.

Even in remote and barren places on earth, God is always present. The difference one person can make with the Lord working through them, even against overwhelming odds, is astounding. There is no limit to what God can accomplish through one willing person. Like a tiny plant growing and eventually breaking a rock.

With confidence in God's power, we can work daily anywhere in the world knowing that we are never alone.

A Labour of Love, a Gift of Peace

Many years ago my husband and I bought an old, small, rundown cottage situated on an overgrown, unkempt piece of land which was surrounded by forest. The property faced a lake reservoir throughout spring and summer, then, during the fall months, it drained to only a dry lakebed in front of our cottage for the winter months. We both thought the property had great potential for beauty.

Before we moved in, I drove alone to the site, stood on the ground and thanked the Lord for leading me to this place. I then asked God to help me turn this little parcel of land into a refuge of peace for all who might set foot there.

And so began our labour of love with sweat and toil, shovel, rake and clippers, work gloves, a wheelbarrow and a dream. We had little money but my husband had a job and I had lots of time. My recently-widowed father also spent one day a week helping us.

We trimmed the trees and shrubs, made a fire-pit, gathered and burned the dead trees and fallen branches. We built a large compost area and filled it with debris refuse. We cut the grass and dug flowerbeds throughout the site, adding to them any flower plants found growing in the lawn. I transplanted wildflowers from the woods and perennial flowers given to us by neighbours and friends. We made walking paths through the surrounding forest and took stock of the special treasures uncovered there including ancient stumps, moss, lichen and mushrooms. We cleared the land of rocks and built two stone walls from them.

My father spent time making birdhouses from scraps of old lumber. We mounted the birdhouses on poles and also hung them on tree branches around the property. As we watched the beauty unfold, I often thanked God for the peace this work brought to my soul.

Years passed and I began to hear comments from visitors, remarking on how peaceful the place was. They would often wander around the lawn, lost in thought while looking at flowers and birdhouses. The children would run through the paths in the forest and I could point out special things along the way.

Men would remark on my father's ability to build a free-standing stone wall with straight sides using no mortar. They were amazed at his skill at eighty-eight years of age, not knowing the construction of the stone wall was also Dad's first attempt. Women would be fascinated by the many different flowers blooming and ask me for cuttings or seeds. I always gave them freely.

We would sit on our deck facing the receding lakefront and changing landscape, watching a great blue heron flying past or a fish jumping out of the water with a splash; butterflies fluttering and bumblebees buzzing from flower to flower; dragonflies catching insects in midflight and kingfishers diving underwater to nab small fish. We heard birds singing in the surrounding forest, geese flying overhead in V formations; saw robins tugging on a worm or hopping across the grass and squirrels dashing to and fro, jumping among the tree branches.

People would speak again of the peace, serenity and beauty around them. I continually thanked God for the paradise He had let me envision and create for others to enjoy. What a blessing this parcel of land had become for all! It reminded me that people can bloom wherever they are planted and be used by God for good no matter what their circumstances.

Sitting in a Bog

Sitting in a bog, searching on a log,
Sitting in a bog, just lookin' for a frog!

A mass of thick willows, how would we get through?
With the wonderful rowboat of Judy and Sue!

Judy struggled with oars floating us between logs.
With hands grabbing branches, we moved through the bog.

We pushed, pulled and prodded, floating this way and that,
Ducking our head but not losing our hat.

The Canada geese seemed to know it was us,
They were honking and flapping, all making a fuss.

The females were nesting quite hidden from view,
'Till along came the rowboat with Judy and Sue.

One female goose was as still as could be,
Sitting well camouflaged at the base of a tree.

We floated quite close, with cameras in hand,
Taking zoomed-in photos without touching land.

Much closer to shore in the midst of the bog,
To our great delight we heard a bullfrog!

We scanned the debris between shoreline and boat
To watch for a movement of froggy afloat

Then moved with great care to a much better scene.
But then we heard croaking from where we had been.

One speedy movement did catch our sharp eye,
But, alas, it was only a blue dragonfly.

The bullfrog was smart, it kept right out of sight,
And rested its voice to croak more through the night.

We had lots of fun, laughs and memories too.
Our latest adventure of Judy and Sue.

The Piercing Truth

My three-year old granddaughter slowly moved her fingers through the dirt in the garden. She lifted a large clump of soil and grabbed at something underneath it. "I caught one, Grandma." She laughed and carefully pulled a long earthworm out of its earthen hole. "Wow! It's a big one!" she said. "It's perfect." I said. "Now we can catch a small fish to put in the water barrel."

I thought back a few years to an interesting conversation I'd had with a forest ranger. I mentioned how wonderful it was to have barrels of rainwater, filled to the brim every rainy day from the cottage eaves-troughs and told him how much better the flowers grew when nourished from warm barrel rainwater than cold well-water.

"My only complaint," I said to him, "is the abundance of mosquitoes around our cottage." They lived part of their lives as larvae in the barrels of motionless water and then ultimately hatched into adult mosquitoes. "Well, I can help you there," he said. "If you catch a small fish in the lake, just put it into the water barrel for a few days and the fish will eat all the mosquito larvae. That's one of their natural foods."

And so began a summer tradition at the cottage. Every week, using a small hook and worm, I would go fishing. Little fish love eating worms as much as they love mosquito larvae, and in a few minutes I'd be pulling a small fish out of the lake. I would keep it in a pail of water until arriving back at the cottage and then transfer it into one of the rain barrels.

It was fascinating watching the fish swim around grabbing the mosquito larvae which wiggled their way toward the surface for air. In a few days the water had not one insect in it. I would then take a small net, catch the fish again and transfer it back into the lake. Mission accomplished. Job well done. No more mass of mosquitoes flying around the cottage waiting for the opportunity to bite some unsuspecting person—like me.

The following week I caught another minnow and repeated the process. My grandchildren loved watching what they referred to as their 'pet' fish. They would quietly tiptoe up to the barrel, then carefully peek over the edge. Suddenly we'd hear, "I see it! Wow! Isn't it a nice fish!"

My reminiscing ended and I took the worm from Crista and pricked it with the tip of the hook, then threaded the worm onto the steel. "Oh, you're hurting it!" Crista moaned. "Is it dying?"

"Its fine, honey," I said with my conscience pricking me as much as I was the worm. "As long as it's wiggling, it's not dead." And with that statement, I cast the worm on the hook out into the water of the lake.

"You watch the floating bobber," I said to Crista. "When it starts to move or bounce, it means a fish is biting the hook." The statement wasn't quite accurate but it sounded better than the truth that the fish was biting the worm. My conscience jabbed me again. Ouch!

My granddaughter just stood there with a worried expression on her dear little face. Out in the water the bobber sat motionless, unusual because our shallow bay was teeming with small fish who loved worms. In a few minutes the tot said, "Grandma, could we check on the worm?"

"Of course," I said and held the fishing pole, letting her reel the bait in to shore. For heaven's sake, I thought, it's just a worm! My conscience pricked me again. She lifted the hook out of the water and there was the worm, wiggling away with no pieces missing.

"See, it's fine." I said, but actually I thought it quite odd. Not one fish had taken a bite. I checked to make sure the sharp tip of the hook was hidden inside the worm, then cast it back out into the water. My granddaughter stood there silent and somber. She wasn't enjoying this event at all.

I again thought back in time. Ever since she was a toddler, we had been teaching her to be kind and gentle with all God's creatures. Whether a puppy or a snail, she was to touch it softly and not hurt it. I was proud of how interested she was in nature, and look what I was doing to that worm! To her, the earthworm was as important as the fish or even the mosquito larvae. They were all holy creations and the way my granddaughter felt about them was right.

I glanced at the motionless bobber and was thankful for the lesson. Then bending down to my despondent granddaughter I said, "Shall we let the worm go now?" Her face lit up with a big smile, her eyes shining with happiness. "Oh yes, Grandma, lets!" she said with relief.

Her faith in me was restored and I silently thanked God, vowing to buy a harmless minnow trap to catch the small fish with bread instead of hooks from now on.

Look Up

God put beauty everywhere if we just look around,
The bees and birds all in the air; the foliage on the ground.

God gave to us a rainbow and skies of purest blue,
White puffy clouds and rays of sun to dry up nightly dew.

God gave us colour, gave us light; then gave us dark to rest,
But we just go our earthly way and miss all but the best.

We walk outside and go to work, complaining as we go,
Too hot, too cold, too windy, too dry, too wet, more snow!

Why are we all so foolish that we cannot raise our eyes,
And marvel at God's treasures all around us like a prize.

In Search of the Great Blue Heron
for Judy Bagnell

Judy came 'round the cottage, her laugh you could hear.
Red hat on her head, extra film in her gear.
Two cameras were ready but the zoom lens was small,
Judy wanted a BIG ONE - maybe buy it this fall.
We pushed off from shore in my rowboat for two,
Our mission today was to find the Great Blue.
Judy sat with the oars and started to row.
I watched from the back telling which way to go.
We headed across the far end of the lake,
Toward the old bridge for some pictures to take.
My eyes scanned the shoreline and floating debris,
For fishing lures tangled sometimes we would see.
Judy'd say, "Oh, I see it!" and row with such zest,
Through brush, weeds and branches - a stamina test.
We also found logs and stumps that would float,
Then drag them aboard, or tie them to the boat.
We both would be standing, pulling with all our might,
Hilarious laughter, we were quite a sight!
Then spied the Great Heron, elusive as ever,
Standing in weeds without moving a feather.
Ready to strike with lightning speed,
A nearby small minnow on which it would feed.
Judy lunged for her camera, knocking it in the boat,
While I grabbed both oars just to keep us afloat.
Then I rowed to get closer, Judy tried to stay steady,
But the Heron took off before she was ready!
We rowed back to my cottage, had a wonderful day,
And there stood the Heron, fishing right in our bay!

Snail Tale

Our granddaughter and her mother were spending the weekend with us at our cottage. It was late spring and the wonderful warm weather made everyone try to spend most of the daylight hours outdoors. Although only three years old, the little tot was fascinated with all God's living things that crept, crawled, slithered or hopped along the ground. She was intent upon picking up anything she found alive.

Because of recent wet weather, there were many ground snails visible around the cottage. You could see them clinging awkwardly to a leaf or working their way laboriously up the wall of the cottage. At night those snails were notorious for sucking the vitality out of my beautiful flowers in various flowerbeds and gardens throughout the property. I didn't tell her that most of the snails I found were pitched as far into the forest as I could throw them. They may be unusual to look at and have pretty striped shells, but those facts didn't make up for the destruction these pests caused to my plants.

Other preferred places where our granddaughter liked to hunt for creatures was under loose pieces of bark clinging to the outside of old logs in our woodpile. She would pry up the bark and inspect the small worms, sow bugs, centipedes and occasional slugs. Centipedes ran very fast and she was unable to keep them in her hand. A slug on the other hand was one of her favorites and she would hold it within her fist until the inside of her hand was covered with its' slime. Undaunted, she peered intently at the slug and questioned where it's eyes, ears and legs were - queries even Grandma had trouble answering, nature lover that she was.

On her previous visit to the cottage, our granddaughter carried a sow bug around in her hand for most of the day. Her Grandma and mother tried valiantly to keep all these creatures out of the cottage, but when the tot left, Grandma looked carefully all around inside of the home to be sure she and Grandpa were truly alone.

This weekend, the child was concentrating on the snails and slugs. She had been carrying a snail around balanced on her right palm. The snail kept sticking out its head equipped with four feelers which protruded independently of each other. As soon as a feeler pushed out, the girl would touch its tip and the snail would pull it back in. When another feeler would jut out, she would touch the end of it too. This became a game with her continually touching the ends of feelers so the snail didn't have time to sense or smell anything. Poke, poke, poke.

The snail began to slide its bulk across her palm and the toddler carefully watched it's movements as the three of us walked across the lawn. Suddenly she grabbed the snail and pulled it right out of its shell.

"Look," she beamed at us happily. "Now I have a slug!" Her mom was horrified!

"Oh No!" she cried, "You can't do that! It's a snail!"

"No. Now it's a slug," the little tot said with determination in her voice. Her mom went into her descriptive, smart-parent mode and began explaining the difference between a slug and a snail. She was clear to let the little girl know that they were not the same creatures and the snail was always supposed to stay in its house.

Our granddaughter stood innocently listening with a slight smile. The knowing look on her face told us she had already accomplished exactly what she'd intended.

Loud Whisperings

I was walking alone beside the Atlantic Ocean one afternoon, on a wide, flat beach that stretched as far in front of me as I could see. The tide was ebbing, leaving occasional small pools of water in indentations on the sand which the rolling waves had once covered but now couldn't reach. It would be many hours before the incoming tide arrived again at this level on the beach.

As the minutes passed, these pools slowly soaked into the beach sand leaving no trace of their previous existence. I strolled slowly along, carefree, enjoying the beautiful sunny day.

Occasionally I picked up a shark's tooth or stopped to admire the vivid colours of wet seashells shining underwater in the puddles. They were so beautiful compared to the dull hues of the dry, sun-bleached shells lying on the hot sand.

At one long puddle, I paused for a moment to watch a three-inch long minnow swimming casually to and fro. On and on I walked, trying not to let my conscience bother me about the inevitable plight of that tiny fish. Dramas like that happened all the time. One minnow of probably thousands stranded daily, slowly running out of water, then gasping and struggling frantically to stay alive while breathing air, but eventually dying on top of the sand as the puddle of water soaked away to nothingness.

The defenseless minnow would be easy food for a sharp-eyed seagull. The fish's death a brutal but natural part of life. Insignificant. Trivial. No one would even know or be concerned about the demise of this wee fish.

My conscience became heavier and more imploring and my footsteps slowed, then finally stopped. I was caught in a silly conundrum. I alone knew the coming fate of this specific minnow.

By that time I had walked a long way up the beach, far from that trifling fish. I turned and stood looking back. Many pools had already disappeared. They had changed shape while soaking away and now looked unfamiliar to what I remembered when passing by them. The minnow was probably already dead. There were many seagulls standing on the sand; hungry birds alert to any sign of struggling life which could fill their stomachs.

I silently argued with myself, an internal war raging. *Why bother even looking for it? Who cares? What difference does the existence of one fish make?* But the truth was, if by chance that minnow was still alive, nothing, not any circumstance, could save its life but me.

I decided my stroll along the beach had gone far enough. I would go home the same route, retracing my footsteps, but I was still not willing to acknowledge the reason why.

There were fewer puddles on the sand now. I glanced at each one for the minnow as I passed by. A plan formed in my mind of how the fish could be captured if I did happen to find it still alive. My footsteps quickened.

I reached the last puddle without finding it, but also recalled I hadn't recognized the shape of that specific long puddle in passing. It was too late - and yet, I remembered the water seemed fairly deep where the fish was swimming. Maybe I had missed seeing the little minnow!

This, I thought, *was just ridiculous! I should leave the beach and go home. I was getting tired. It would soon be time to cook supper. Hadn't I already looked at each puddle? Could I have tried harder and been more thorough*? I did remember seeing some floating debris on a couple of pools. Maybe the minnow had been swimming underneath something and was out of sight as I walked by.

Precious time was being wasted while standing there arguing with myself. I just had to look for that little minnow one more time!

A sense of urgency overtook me as I again made my way back up the beach from puddle to puddle checking carefully.

Lo and behold! There it was swimming back and forth, already struggling and seemingly terrified in the quickly shallowing water. Hastily I put my plan into action. I knelt down near one end of the puddle and pushed sand up to make a dam, while leaving a small pool of water on the other side of the dam.

I left a narrow channel between the pools. The fish sensed my presence and swam around in a frenzy, continually avoiding the new dam. It hid under a floating piece of wood. The minnow was so tiny I thought, a seagull wouldn't even consider it a snack. Or would it? A curious bold gull landed on the sand close by and stood watching.

My knees hurt from the sharp pieces of broken seashells embedding themselves into my skin as I slowly leaned forward and herded the fish toward the dam. The poor little minnow would surely die of stress if it wasn't caught soon!

This time it swam through the channel into the smaller pool. I pushed the sand dam above water level; carefully scooped up the small minnow in my hands; struggled to my feet and ran across the sand to the ocean. I gently lowered the wiggling minnow into the water. With a swish of its tail, the wee fish disappeared into the wave, free at last.

Success! I had saved it! I was thrilled and delighted! To do right was worth every effort; every step I had taken and every instant of time spent in the quest. With a smiling face, a thankful heart and a bouncing step, I left the beach.

And do you know, in all those many puddles on the beach that day, only one puddle held one minnow for me to save, or not.

Joy and Thankfulness

Appreciation

Thank you God for giving us the chance of another day,
Thank you Lord for listening to the things we have to say.
Thank you for our sight, so we can read what has been learned,
Thank you for our mind to understand what's been discerned.
Thank you for our souls that we may grow with each new day,
Thank you for Your Son, whose earthly life showed us the way.

Cancer Scare

When I was in my mid-fifties, I became increasingly short of breath over the period of a few months. I went to my family doctor who ordered chest x-rays and a CT scan which revealed a tumour the size of an orange inside my left lung. More tests confirmed it was cancer and in order to save my life the surgeon had to remove my whole left lung. The tumour had started to metastasize and had already infected a lymph node within the same lung.

I also had a lung disease in my right lung but it wasn't cancer. Although progressive over time, it could be mainly controlled by inhalers and medication. I was so thankful that God had given me more time on earth. Life was put into perspective of what was truly important – the gift of more time to love and help others and be a positive influence on my children, grandchildren, friends and serve the Lord any way I could.

As time passed my surgical incision healed and I learned how to slow my daily activities down and function with the air capacity of the one diseased lung remaining.

Every morning I thank God for a new day and ask to be a blessing to everyone I have contact with. This prayer has made my life rich and full. It inspires me to be joyful in all circumstances.

> Thank you Lord for giving me the chance of another day. I give my will today to You, may Thy will be done in my life. Please help me be a blessing to all those I have contact with. May You use me for Your glory and may the Holy Spirit take away my selfishness and teach me how to be humble – to put the thoughts and needs and welfare of others ahead of myself. I ask in Jesus' name, Amen.

This simple prayer every morning has given me the strength and optimism to be cheerful and keep my day in perspective for God. Nearly two decades have now passed and my cancer scare has been transformed into a blessing.

My Daily Prayer

Thank you Lord for giving me
A golden opportunity
To edify You through this day,
In all I do and what I say.

For yesterday is over now,
Tomorrow's not in view,
So guide me through the present time,
I give today to You.

Peace

In a world unsure and torn,
In a stable dark, forlorn,
To a maiden tired and worn,
God's son Jesus Christ was born.

Shepherds heard the heavens rejoice,
Angels sang with holy voice.
"Glory to God" their sounds did call,
"Peace on earth, goodwill to all."

Something sacred happened here,
Angels told them not to fear,
All were guided by a star,
Shepherds, then wise men from afar.

Two thousand years have passed away,
Since Jesus in a manger lay,
Those words, still true, as towers fall,
"Peace on earth, goodwill to all."

Hatred causes us to fall,
Love however, conquers all.

Pathways

When I look out across the sky on a mostly cloudy day,
I see the shafts of sunlight beaming to the ground in a way
That reminds me of what prayer is like when we seek the Lord above.
Our thoughts are like a beam of light from the earth to God of Love.

By gazing at these sunbeams, I turn them all around,
Instead of shining toward the earth, they rise up from the ground.
I imagine all God's people as far as the eye can see,
Sending prayers in rays of light in praise and thanks to Thee.

Faith

The Beginning
Based on - Matthew 7:7 and 8

Hello God - are you there?
It's me - Sue Gordon.
Actually, I'm Susan Grace Alton Dolderman Gordon.
Do you know me?
I want to find you.
I need to know if you're real.
Can I talk to you like this?
The prayers I know don't seem to mean much to me.
Someone else made them up.
I want to find you myself.
Amen.

Hello God - it's me again.
Susan Alton Dolderman Gordon.
Can you help me?
I'm such a mess!
My whole life's a mess.
Do I mean anything to you?
I have to find out if you're there.
Can you let me know somehow?
Amen.

Hello God - it's me again.
Susan Gordon.
I don't know what else to do so I guess I'll just start talking to you.
I hope you can hear me.
I hope you are real.
I need to find you.
I'll just start telling you about myself.
Amen.
- and on I went.

A Purpose in Life

Do your best each hour of the day,
Help those you can who pass your way,
Give a smile, a cheery word to whomever you see,
For compassion and joy there is no fee.

Be thankful for where you've been placed on earth,
For the gifts you've been given to reveal your worth,
Fruits of the Spirit, peace in your soul,
Patience, goodness and self-control.

Forgive the ones who have blocked your way,
As forgiveness strengthens your soul each day,
The body wastes and is finally gone,
But your soul evolves and goes on and on.

Be Prepared

A winter storm came upon us during the night with high winds, cold temperatures, blowing snow. The electric power went out, then came back on. My husband and I immediately got out of bed and prepared for the possibility of the power going off again. I made coffee early, filling my husband's thermos and also making his lunch for work. We filled many pails with water for use in the bathroom and kitchen and also found candles and matches if required.

The power went off again and stayed out for hours. We then rested, comforted that whatever possible had already been done to prepare ourselves for the duration of the storm.

By comparing this story to our faith in God, it reminded me that we must not put things off to some future time. We should try consistently to be prepared for the coming storms in life or the possibility of Jesus' return at an unknown hour.

The Balloon

I have always had difficulty letting go of my problems. I would ask the Lord to look after them but then I'd get another idea and try something else on my own. Eventually one problem was beyond my control. All efforts were futile and the burden was heavy on my shoulders.

My daughter gave me a helium balloon for my birthday and during that night I had a wonderful idea. Early the next morning I took the balloon outside. Gripping the balloon's string tightly, I directed my thoughts and prayers to God. I mentally placed the burden of my problem on that balloon and then let go of the string. Up into the sky it sailed and I could feel the heavy burden lifting from my shoulders as the balloon rose higher and higher toward the heavens.

The Ladder Bookmark

It's made of plastic canvas
And then crocheted with love.
To become a bookmark symbol,
For remembering God above.

For me it's like a ladder,
To climb toward the Cross,
With rungs of truth to cling to
And sustain us during loss.

Each step becomes a lesson
We learn throughout our life.
Patience, kindness, faithfulness,
Battling hate and strife.

The goal is Jesus on the cross,
Who died for all our sin.
The ultimate end - eternal life
If we just let Him in.

So, thank you for the bookmark,
A useful gift, you see.
And I will cherish it because
It means so much to me.

The Answer

Thank you Lord for doubt, which sneaks into my mind.
It gives me the incentive to try harder then to find the
answers to those questions upon which I struggle so,
Then finally realize - with faith,
I just don't need to know.

The Knot for Life

Some days we are weary and tired of the strife,
When doubt gets a foothold in our mind.
Are we really falling and not in our calling?
Or doubt hid the truth and made us blind?

As you slide down the rope just don't lose hope,
There's a knot at the bottom to hang on to.
'Till the storm subsides, let God be your guide,
He'll help you hang on - if you want to.

If you're all uptight and you've lost the light,
For your way has become a dead end,
Only peace you need but not sin and greed,
Then come to the Lord my friend.

As you slide down the rope, just don't lose hope,
There's a knot at the bottom to hang on to.
'Till the storm subsides, let God be your guide,
He'll help you hang on - if you want to.

Spiritual Warfare

The Armour of God

Arise in the morning and pray to God,
Prepare yourself for war.
The devil knows you're a Christian now,
You were no threat before.

Stand your ground when evil comes,
Put on the belt of truth,
The breastplate of God's righteousness,
Feet planted, as in youth.

Adjust your helmet of salvation,
Jesus overcame the world.
Hold firm your shield of faith in God,
Christ's banner is now unfurled.

The sword of the Holy Spirit in you,
God's Word of Truth shall reign.
For satan's fate is in God's plan,
When Christ shall come again.

This is not a massive invasion,
Of satan's evil domain,
But individual soldiers of God,
Withstanding the devil's reign.

Character of God will win the war,
Not brute force when it's tense.
For a Christian's character is in God's Strength,
And it's our best defense.

Be alert and always pray
For other Christians too.
Which gives them strength for their own need,
Fighting evil as you do.

Arise in the morning and pray to God,
Prepare yourself for war.
The devil knows you're a Christian now,
You were no threat before.

A Choice to Make

I felt my blood pressure rising,
And fought hard to hold back a tear,
For an old, old lie had been whispered
To my granddaughter's innocent ear.

I was tempted to defend my position,
And bring the old story to light,
But I can't win alone against satan,
Even though my defense was right.

Retaliation is not the answer,
For satan then becomes the boss.
So I gathered my hateful, unspoken thoughts,
And left them all at the foot of the Cross.

To deal with untruths, just go forward,
And continue to worship the Lord.
For Jesus overcame this life's evils,
And we live secure in God's Word.

Helping Others

Ultimate Power

For twenty years my husband and I owned and operated a school bus company. My seventy-two passenger bus route covered many miles in a rural community and the children ranged from three-year-olds in junior kindergarten to eighteen-year old students attending their last year of high school.

What a diverse mixture it was, all those ages, from every economic background, impoverished to wealthy, sitting together for three hours each school day.

There were some children that disliked each other and had to be seated apart from their current "enemies of the day." It was a constant demand to keep peace and concentrate on driving safely.

For many years I had the challenge of one particular student named Fred, disliked by every student on the bus. Fred lived in a shack. He wore old hand-me-down clothes, had no socks to wear in the cold Canadian winter and had a chip on his shoulder as big as a log. With three older brothers and not enough supplies to go around the family, Fred learned at an early age to fight for whatever he wanted with whomever he wanted it from. He not only had to wrestle and throw punches, but yell, swear and be the most vicious if he was to have a chance of winning.

This behavior did not work out well on a moving school bus. Fred didn't fit in at all with the other students. No one wanted to sit beside him. Most children near his age were afraid of him, and with good reason. Fred was a time-bomb of anger just waiting to be ignited. The wrong look or a thoughtless word, and he would explode into action – yelling, kicking and punching to get even.

Many times I had to pull the school bus over to the side of the road and physically block Fred in a seat with my sheer size, clear the students from around him, and slowly talk his rage out so he could regain control of himself. Then we would continue the bus route.

Fred's parents were unable to transport him to school. The school had their own problems with him and Fred must attend. He was only a young boy of eight and needed education. His rages happened four or five times a year, not often enough for any permanent transportation changes to be made, so Fred remained on my bus and the years passed by.

I sympathized with Fred. He was a boy with an uncontrollable temper caused mostly by his circumstances in life of which he had no control. He tried to be good and desperately wanted to be like the other kids. He wanted friends but sometimes he "snapped." I treated him equally and would back Fred up if he was unfairly accused. Because of my attitude, he liked me, trusted me and respected my authority on the bus. I prayed a lot for guidance and wisdom in dealing with this boy, and always asked God to watch over me when driving the school bus.

A cloud of worry would sometimes descend on my mind. What if Fred loses control and really hurts someone before I have time to stop him? What if his outburst distracts me causing an accident? How will I control Fred when he's as large as I am? God would always bring me back into perspective. Take one day at a time, one incident at a time. Trust in the Lord to guide me.

As time went on, Fred grew bigger, stronger and developed more long-time enemies on the bus. I felt with dread that some unmanageable incident was creeping closer.

Then one day, it happened! Fred picked on a much older, larger boy. All my public school children were on the bus. I was parked at the high school waiting for the teenagers to board the bus, be seated and then we would leave the school at 3:30p.m. It was 3:25p.m.

A fifteen-year-old boy named Andy climbed the steps and started down the aisle while carrying an armload of school books. Fred stuck his foot out causing Andy to trip over it and fall flat on the floor in the aisle. In an instant Andy jumped up, grabbed Fred, threw him into the aisle and was on top of him beating Fred with his fists.

Time passed in slow-motion as I undid my seatbelt, lunged out of the seat and charged down the aisle, telling the boys to stop fighting. They paid no attention of course. Everyone scrambled to clear the aisle and seats around them. The first thing to do was separate the unmatched boys.

I grabbed Andy by the back of his coat, and with adrenalin pumping, lifted him out of the aisle, twisting him into the seat on my left as I put myself between the two boys. Taking my hands off Andy's coat, I held up my left hand staring at it. A dead silence pervaded the whole bus. My wedding ring finger was dislocated at the large joint, twisted upside-down and was sticking sideways across my little finger. The silence was deafening! Fred and Andy's mouths hung open in shock!

Because of my previous prayer to God, I was completely calm and said, "Look what has happened because of you two boys fighting." Utter silence! The scuffle was over and the damage had been done to me instead of one of them. They were devastated!

Twenty-five buses were all pulling out of the school parking lot. It was 3:30p.m. and everyone was moving but me. There was no time to find another driver. I said another prayer for God to help me stay calm and drive safely. Fred got off the floor and sat down in a daze. I sat down, did up my seat belt and started driving one of the quietest bus routes of my career.

During the next one and one-half hours, the students were delivered home by me—and the Lord. I drove with my left wrist gripping the steering wheel as I shifted gears and opened and closed the bus doors with my right hand at each child's stop. I kept looking at my finger, amazed that there was no pain and I was so calm.

The bus was finally empty. I drove home, got in my car and drove another twenty minutes to the hospital. The pain started in the hospital parking lot.

My finger was broken in three places and dislocated at the large joint. The broken bone was too tiny to correct with pins, so the finger is permanently bent forward at the little joint, and a bit turned to the left. Every time I notice it, which is often, I thank the Lord for leading me safely that day and for keeping the pain away while I concentrated on driving. I had no hard feelings—it was an accident. I explained to the boys my broken finger wasn't their fault, but it was the result of their actions fighting. It was a sobering lesson for them.

Andy moved out of my bus area shortly afterwards, but for years to come, always made a point of speaking to me whenever we met and I always saw him glance at my crooked finger.
The shock of realizing his fighting had caused the only person he liked on the school bus to get hurt had a tremendous effect on Fred. During the next two years of riding my bus, he was never involved in trouble again.

My faith in God and His ultimate power was definitely strengthened that day.

First Things First

It was hard for me to grasp the reality that I had lung cancer. I was in no pain and felt good except being more tired and short of breath when active. However, those symptoms were enough for me to ask my family doctor for chest x-rays and breathing tests because I didn't feel quite right.

The x-ray showed a large tumour within the left lung. Further tests revealed that it was cancer. At least part of my lung would have to be removed as soon as possible.

My first concern was telling my husband and three children, to include them in every instant of my remaining existence. Then to tell my neighbours and close friends, plus asking to be put on a prayer chain list of which I'm a member. These people were my support group and I was confident I would be uplifted and carried by their prayers.

On the day of the tests before the lung operation, after all the forms were filled out, I sat in a pre-op area among six other people, all strangers, three men and three women. Following previous instruction sheets, the ladies wore no makeup, no jewelry, had endured the fasting and were wearing hospital gowns covered by housecoats and slippers.

The exception was one woman decked out in earrings, necklace, bracelets, rings, and wearing enough eye-shadow, rouge, mascara and lipstick to last me a year. I don't think she could face the possibility of being in a public place without her makeup or jewelry.

One man wore a housecoat of greatly outdated velour fabric, undoubtedly saved for the possibility of a hospital stay at some point during his lifetime. The other two men look very uncomfortable in yellow hospital wraps, their bare feet in old, worn running shoes.

We were certainly objects of interest to observe. I was determined not to spend money on anything new for such a serious occasion. I sat in the heat of May wearing an old cotton housecoat and my only slippers which were warm, ankle length, fuzzy black booties. The lady beside me was adorned in an elaborate satin housecoat with matching pink satin slippers. She looked lovely.

It occurred to me that the six of us were all reduced to the same common denominator— people in hospital attire, all awaiting surgery of one kind or another. There was nothing in any of our circumstances of life that could change the fact that, rich or poor, male or female, old or young, black, white, Asian or of other colour, here we all were together, sitting in a small hospital cubicle awaiting an operation.

One man looked like he would be much more comfortable wearing a suit and tie. Many sat silently, wrapped within their own thoughts. I complimented the lady with the beautiful satin housecoat. She was pretty, even without makeup, with long natural blonde hair, slim and trim as they say and possibly in her early forties. She seemed happy to have someone to talk to. She was waiting to have two lumps removed from one breast. I sensed the worry. We chatted together as if alone.

Her name was Maria. She smiled and said she went by the name Mary. A nurse appeared and called her name. We wished each other well as she left to begin her medical journey. An hour later I watched a nurse place Mary's pretty satin housecoat and pink slippers in a plastic bag. I knew her operation had begun and prayed to the Lord silently for peace and comfort for Mary.

In those circumstances, there was no more we strangers could do for each other. But the greatest help we can be to anyone is to pray, interceding for them and asking God to surround and support them with love, comfort and healing during their time of need. That is our part. God will take care of the rest.

Through the Ages

I read the day's devotions
When my granddaughter was here.
Though she was only five years old
And to her it wasn't clear.

She knew it was important,
Something Grandma did each day.
To read of God who loves us,
And what He has to say.

And though I may not be here
When she grows up someday,
I pray that she'll remember,
Grandma trusted God each day.

Small Steps Forward

She didn't get to Church very often but this particular Sunday had a chance to attend. After great deliberation on what to wear, not having many 'good clothes,' off she went, contemplating. *Okay Lord, here I come. I hope the sermon's good so I can learn something, and I'd like to know the songs too. I need to open my mind to becoming a better Christian.*

She chose the Salvation Army church and walked in thinking she'd better sit in a spot by herself so that she could concentrate.

A family with four little girls entered and sat directly in front of her. She hoped they would be quiet. Their mother turned around and visited. Of course she mentioned that it was hard to decide what to wear as it was a hot day. The lady replied, "Oh we're glad to have you in any kind of clothing! The Lord accepts you just as you are! Boy, she had that coming – first lesson learned.

Then a man entered and plopped down beside her. He looked at her with drool on his chin, spoke a few unintelligible words then sat waiting for her reply. The lady in front said that he usually sat with another couple who weren't there yet and she could move to another seat if she wanted to. She chose to stay rather than bring attention to her situation.

She looked at him and asked, "What did you say?" He had beautiful light brown eyes and smiled. "Whadawedonow? Whadawedonow?" She caught it – oh Joy! What do we do now?

"Just sit and wait," she said, "We'll sing soon." So there they sat, him and her, waiting.

The smell of urine was overpowering! Possibly he was in adult diapers. She prayed to the Lord to help keep her from gagging. God did help her. She didn't gag.

The service began and the first hymn was announced. She took a hymn book and found the proper page. He just sat there. So she got another hymn book, found the page, pointed to the beginning and gave it to him. They stood.

She sang. He stared at the book, but was quiet and good. Her heart filled with tenderness for him.

And so it went, throughout the service. He couldn't read. He couldn't sing, but he could hold the book and she had him at the right page.

It was time for the offering. She had her money. He was searching all his pockets – nothing! He took out a wallet; opened it – nothing! He found an ADMIT ONE ticket but the lady holding the collection plate said, "No. You keep that." Meanwhile she had also been digging in her purse, then handed him a dollar. He smiled and put it in the collection plate and the service continued.

She heard the whole sermon. The children in front were quiet and coloured in books. Their parents were loving and bringing the girls up in a Christian atmosphere. Jesus said, *"Let the little children come to me and do not forbid them; for of such is the kingdom of God"* (Mark 10:pt.14 NKJV).

The captain in his Sermon, mentioned that some people are afflicted, and all you can do is stand beside them. That's right. This man beside her will go to Heaven and be whole again. She will be judged for how she treated him on earth because she is whole now.

He asked her many times, "Whadawedonow?" and was always content with the answer. The last time he asked, she said, "It's time to go home." And with that, he jumped up and left.

She didn't find out his name, but learned so much that day. God knows what we need to learn and in what order. We don't. What we are to do is ask the Lord for knowledge with an open mind and then learn by what takes place before us. *"Nevertheless not My will, but Yours, be done"* (Luke 22:pt.42 NKJV). The unexpected in our eyes may happen exactly as the Lord has intended. She used to think life was sometimes dull, repetitive and depressing. Now every day is exciting if she concentrates on learning.

The Awesome Power of Prayer

I woke up hoping to accomplish some great thing for the Lord,
But no extravaganza lit up my mental board.

So then I thought, if nothing special happens to me today,
What can I do to help and serve my Father anyway?

I can pray for all the people in the world who are in need,
And I can supplicate for those who concentrate on greed.

I can pray for someone who is sick, or crippled, or in pain,
Or people who are blinded by materialistic gain.

I can ask for comfort to surround someone weighed down by grief,
To ease the burden in their heart and give them some relief.

For prayer is like a beacon of brilliant, shining light,
Beaming straight to God, our Father, whether day or night.

So this is what I'll do today, pray throughout each hour,
For I know truly in my heart, that prayer is awesome power.

Nudges

    Here was another Church bulletin in my mailbox! I knew they were periodically left by my Christian friend. Sometimes I was annoyed getting this mail, but usually I read the stories in the bulletin which prompted me to ponder the meaning of faith and think about religion.
    When I was searching for God, a wise Christian once told me that Jesus would surround me with other Christian people to help and guide me. And I realized that was exactly what was happening with these Church bulletins in my mailbox.
    I am forever grateful to my friend for her loving nudges and now try daily to pass on goodness to others. You never know all the times that God uses you to influence other people in a Christian way without you even realizing it.

Choking Ordeal – Seniors Beware

Having only one lung and also a lung disease, I know what it's like to be short of breath and I understand the need to function at a slower pace than other people. However, I wasn't aware of the physical feelings people dealt with in more extreme circumstances, which obscured the cause of my ordeal.

It was early morning. There had been thunderstorms throughout the night and the electric power had been off in our house for six hours by the time we awoke. Usually in that type of weather, we have an air conditioner running to clear the humidity, thereby helping me breathe.

My early-morning routine was to have a coffee, take daily pills, then make my husband's lunch while he showered and got ready to leave the house for work.

Today I felt winded and sluggish but blamed it on the poor air quality in the house. I got a glass of water and tried to swallow the three large calcium pills, one at a time. I often have trouble swallowing these big pills and sometimes gag trying to get them down my throat.

This morning was no different. I tried to swallow the first grey pill but it didn't go down. I swallowed again. It stuck to the roof of my mouth. I swallowed more water. The pill felt rough on my tongue, the outside coating already wearing off. It went down my throat, but I gagged and back up it came. I was getting stressed. Two more pills to take after this one! I swallowed again, gagging at the same time and the pill went down sideways, scraping my throat I thought.

After much coughing and feeling tense, I finally managed to swallow the last two large grey pills.

I proceeded to make my husband's lunch but felt weak, hot and worn out from the pill-swallowing ordeal. I didn't seem to be getting enough air.

This weather is sure taking its toll on me today, I thought. *I can hardly get around the house!* Sitting on a chair, I leaned forward and put my elbows on the table, trying to get more air into my lung.

I was sweating profusely and decided to lie down. Walking the ten steps to the bedroom was exhausting and took more air and energy than I had. Plus difficulty breathing! My diaphragm couldn't expand while lying down so I quickly sat back up on the bed - another mistake. Anxiety began. I panicked and worried about the possibility of becoming unconscious.

Shaking all over, wet with perspiration, I willed myself to not move, to calm down, breathe at a steady pace, and slowly the panic subsided. I thanked God for bringing me out of the anxiety attack, then called my husband from the bathroom.

He lightly patted me a few times between the shoulder blades, blamed my poor breathing on the weather and lack of air conditioning, told me to take it easy and left for work.

I sat still, rested and eventually felt a little better, so got up and made the bed. Such an easy task but immediately the weakness, sweating, stress and anxiety for air returned.

What is happening to me, I thought. *How could my health go downhill so fast? Was I beginning to die?* All my muscles seemed to be shaking. They were screaming for oxygen. I felt very puzzled and confused.

The electric power came back on. Working very slowly I closed all the windows and doors and turned on the air conditioner. Thank goodness that ordeal was over!

But it wasn't. I felt exactly the same, exhausted, shaky, sweating and labouring for air. It took energy to keep my head up, to move my arms and legs; to even turn my head. And I didn't have enough energy.

After three hours of sitting at the table, I was just too tired and had to lie down. If I became unconscious, so be it. I couldn't think clearly, therefore the thought of calling 9-1-1, or a neighbour didn't occur to me.

I staggered to the bedroom, laid down on the bed and felt something move within my throat. Choking, gagging, gasping, I sat up and brought something up into my mouth. A chunk. I spit it into a Kleenex. It was a big, grey pill, softened but still intact and even larger than normal size because it had slowly absorbed water and saliva over a period of now- five hours!

Oxygen flooded my body. I could breathe again! Energy returned. Immediately. It was amazing! Thank God!

The pill had partially blocked the entrance to my only lung, and over that length of time, slowly softened, enlarging even more, thereby blocking still more air from entering my system.

I was very blessed. Many people die from choking or asphyxiation. God has given me a chance to tell this story. Maybe it will help someone be more aware of the symptoms of choking. Maybe drug companies will take heed and limit the size of pills we are expected to swallow.

Maybe the sale of hammers and pill-crushers will rise. And maybe someone's life will be saved by this story.

The Ripple Effect

I tossed a little pebble
In a quiet pool of water,
And watched the waves start rolling from the core.

They started as a circle,
Lined up behind each other,
And marched away toward the distant shore.

And so it is with people,
And how they treat each other,
Whether good or bad, there is the ripple effect.

If you love people as they are,
Good will spread from near to far,
And the world will be improved by your respect.

Valuable Service

"It's not an emergency, but the doctor would like to discuss your x-rays with you as soon as possible. Could you be in our office tomorrow morning at 9:30?"

I instinctively knew something ominous had shown up on my chest x-ray. Fear constricted my throat and I prayed, "Dear Lord, please stay with me through this trial ahead."

A few years ago I had been diagnosed with a lung condition called Chronic Obstructive Pulmonary Disease or COPD, and had controlled the symptoms with regular usage of inhalers since that time. However, during the last six months, I felt my stamina slipping and my breathing weakening. I had recently requested having more x-rays taken to compare with the last set of x-rays a couple of years' previous.

The following morning my husband and I were told the x-ray had shown a large tumour within the left lung. My first thought was to inform my family and also ask to be put on the prayer chain in my Church. I felt a great need to be surrounded by positive support and prayer.

For many years I have felt close to the Lord and under the protection of His love and care. Because of this belief, I have always been confident of the final outcome of my life; only the appointed time of my death remains a mystery.

The next three weeks passed in a blur of medical tests and appointments. The thoracic surgeon stated that at least part of the lung would have to be removed as soon as possible. Without surgery I had one year to live. The operation itself didn't worry me, but I was concerned about whether I could still be useful to God and others afterward.

Upon coming out of the anesthetic, one look at my dear husband's face and I knew that the surgeon had removed my whole lung. The fear of becoming an invalid and dependent upon others gripped me like a vise, but I couldn't remain afraid with so much love and support of prayer surrounding me. I felt so blessed already—if only I could still be useful to the Lord.

I was moved into a hospital room with one other patient, an elderly lady almost twenty years my senior, but in about the same physical condition as me. We both had fresh incisions, multiple tubes, chest drains and were hooked up to oxygen to help us breathe. Her condition however was deteriorating while mine would improve with time. Feeling supported by love and prayer, I immediately introduced myself to her as "her new neighbour."

During the next few days we talked, groaned and even laughed with each other, being included when the other had visitors. Once every day I would be helped into a wheelchair and taken to another floor of the hospital for x-rays. When leaving the room I would tell my neighbour, "Oh the places I'll go and the things I'll see! I'll tell you all my adventures when I return." She'd say, "Have a good trip," and we would both laugh.

Her children told my children what an inspiration and blessing I had been to their mother and how she had thrived since I had been in the room. Then I knew God had answered my fear. Even while lying in a hospital bed He could use us as an instrument of love and peace to the medical staff, other patients and to those in daily contact.

I'm so happy to have been shown that the Lord can use each of us for His good no matter what our circumstances. All we have to do is trust and believe. God will do the rest.

Point of View

It pains to see you look at me with pity in your eyes,
Your embarrassment and awkwardness to me is no surprise.
You don't ask any questions - just try hard not to stare,
All you see is physical, I sit in a wheelchair.

There was a time some years ago when I could jump or run,
Or skate or dance or tippy-toe in circles just for fun.
Those times are still fresh in my mind, although I don't despair,
For I've been given other gifts to use from my wheelchair.

I have the gift of empathy for those weighed down by grief,
And a funny sense of humour to give the sad relief.
I telephone the elderly to let them know I care,
And have a pleasant visit as I sit in my wheelchair.

I once was very angry and cried to God above,
He saved me from this agony by filling me with love.
We're given trials to overcome, my soul to Him stood bare,
The aspiration from the Lord - spread love from my wheelchair.

So don't avert your eyes from me and treat me less than whole,
Acceptance is all that I need to help me reach my goal.
For I have plans and dreams like you and many gifts to share,
A worthwhile life I daily lead though strapped in a wheelchair.

Baby Shoes

When my son was about to get married he told me of the pondering he had done regarding the big change he was making in his life.

I gave him a pair of his baby shoes I had saved all these years to show how many steps he had already taken and how much he had grown from when he wore that first pair of shoes.

In applying that to our spiritual life, we should be thankful when remembering all the steps forward we have taken in our faith and how the Lord has helped us grow throughout the years compared to what we first knew in our faith journey to Jesus.

Now we can pass our knowledge on to our family and others to help them grow in their own lives.

Your Memory of Me

Life is but a journey, we all know how it ends,
So now's the time to live your best with strangers and with friends.

For you will be remembered in a non-material way,
Of how you treated everyone and how you lived each day.

How to Shine Your Light for Others
To Judy from Sue

From hospital visits
To pics of our yard,
Floating roses in bowls
And a cute homemade card.

Nice roll-on deodorant,
A tulip tree bloom,
Your quick wit and smile
Just light up the room.

Unique get-well package,
And laughs from a chair,
Phone calls almost daily,
Slow walks for fresh air.

You've been such a blessing
I'm well on the mend.
Here's a THANK YOU from Sue,
Your neighbour and friend.

Salvation

Wonderful News

Wonderful news, I have wonderful news,
It's never too late - did you know?
That Jesus is waiting for our call to the end,
God loves us that much, it is so.

While Jesus was dying on Calvary's cross,
A man hung beside Him - a thief.
The thief was accepting this fate for his crimes,
But Jesus' innocence was his belief.

The thief knew that Jesus had done nothing wrong,
And he asked of the Lord in his pain,
"Remember me when into Your Kingdom You come,"
Jesus said he'd be with Him again.

Yes, Jesus replied, *"I tell you the truth,*
Today, you will be with Me in Paradise." (Luke 23:43 NIV)
He accepted the thief's soul at the absolute end,
And released him from satan's own vice.

So friend, God can use you right up to the end,
To before you will take your last breath.
To show your family, a nurse or a friend,
You're at peace - and there's more - after death.

God gave you a choice, please don't wait too long,
To have Jesus come into your heart.
He'll enter right then and forgive all your sin,
And you'll finally have a new start.

The Anchor

How do you, on the outside,
Hide what's on the inside,
When the burden is too hard for you to bear?
God sees your very soul,
He alone can make you whole,
So take your trouble to the Lord in prayer.

How can you explain,
The crushing, intense pain,
When no one can perceive or truly care?
Let Jesus be your guide,
In Him you can confide,
Just tell it to the Lord, He's always there.

What a heavy cost,
For people who feel lost,
And carry all their problems on their own.
Please just understand,
That God will take your hand,
And never more will you be all alone.

The Change Within

Glory be to You, oh Lord,
Though I was full of sin.
You have claimed me as Your own,
And come to dwell within.

You've given me great riches Lord,
Of peace within my soul.
And taught me truths I hungered for,
Made me, a sinner, whole.

And now I pray for ones oppressed,
I cry with those who grieve.
And yearn to give support to those
Who do not yet believe.

I know I'll never qualify,
For all You've given me.
My happiness, renewed each day,
In praise and thanks to Thee.

The Door of Life

Don't you know God is waiting for you to knock at the door of Life.
We have a free choice - that was God's will too,
So please put an end to your strife.

Knock at the door, the angels will cheer, another lamb comes to the fold.
Knock at the door, and lose all your fear,
Your soul is more precious than gold.

The door has no latch, you cannot get in by good deeds or money to pay.
You have to believe that Jesus is Lord,
He's waiting for your knock today.

Knock at the door, the angels will cheer, another lamb comes to the fold.
Knock at the door, and lose all your fear,
Your soul is more precious than gold.

God is Real

I read a book the other day that was given to me by a "friend",
Which put the whole Christian theory
To an inconclusive end.

For a while I found this depressing that suspicion slipped quietly in.
But reflecting this point - there's no question at all,
My faith would ultimately win.

For I used to feel utterly lost and alone, and I knew what hate was all about.
I cried for Jesus to rescue me,
And He did, there is no doubt.

Jesus changed my heart of stone I feel,
Gave me peace in the depths of my soul.
God is always near and very real,
Filled the longing I had to be whole.

Jesus gave me great contentment, and others I now can forgive.
I'm changed as sure as I write these words,
That is how I know God surely lives.

Some people may question, is Jesus real,
Search for fault within God's Holy Book.
Circumstances prove the Lord wrong, they feel,
But my heart is wherein I look.

You can challenge the Bible all you want,
And surmise its complexity.
To some people, research may surely taunt,
But Jesus, indeed, lives in me.

Eulogy Comfort

My young sister in law recently passed away from cancer. Her family was devastated, especially the two children still living at home. They had so many events to face in their future without their mother's presence.

She was deaf and couldn't speak for herself, so I decided to communicate my thoughts at the funeral to celebrate her life while on earth. During the eulogy I said that the people we love and lose are no longer where they were before. They are now with us in our memory wherever we are."

What a comforting way for her children to remember their beloved mother. They know she is in heaven with Jesus and her memory is as close as their next thought.

Because of Jesus' resurrection from death on the cross, Jesus is alive and we can ask Him to come into our life and be our personal Saviour. We need not be afraid but be comforted by the fact our death is not final, only a transition from earth to eternal life with God.

Transformation
(An Adult Becoming a Christian)

What my life has become I compare to a tree.
My branches grow as God strengthens me.
And I have been changed for all to see,
I may even bear fruit by helping thee
-- In the future!
                                                                Hallelujah!

Once upon a time I was only a seed,
-- But I was dormant.
                                                             She was dormant.

And I lived half my life just fulfilling my own need,
-- But I stayed dormant.
                                                                 Only dormant.

Now I was surrounded by a hardened shell,
I tried my best, but didn't do too well.
Is there more to life or just a living hell
-- Being dormant?
                                                          Staying dormant?

But then I finally heard someone say,
That God and His Son Jesus Christ are the Way
So, how do I find them? Maybe start to pray
To Jesus Christ. I'll start today!
-- And my shell cracked!
                                              Oh, her shell cracked!

Well, oh Lord, here I am at last,
-- I'm a sinner.

                                                                              She's a sinner!

On my knees, please forgive my past,
-- A broken sinner.

                                                                            Broken sinner!

I've tried every way to run my own life,
There's been nothing but heartache and trouble and strife.
The pain in me is just as sharp as a knife,
-- I'm such a sinner!

                                                                                Such a sinner!

What do I do, Lord? Here's my plight.
I feel too shabby to be in Your sight,
I'm at the end, and I've lost the fight.
And God whispered to me, "Just follow the Light."
-- And my shell broke!

                                                    Lord, her shell broke!

And warmth filled me, Jesus entered in,
-- To my heart.

                                                                              To her heart.

He cast out the sin that had been within,
-- From the start.

                                                                              From the start.

There's no need to mourn, just reason to cheer!
I've been reborn and lost all my fear
The Lord will teach me for He's always near,
-- Hallelujah!

                                             Hallelujah!

I had been living down deep in a hole,
But Jesus had died to save even my soul,
And to show us the way, that was His goal.
In God's Book of Life, I'm now on the roll!
-- And I grew roots!
                                        And she grew roots!

So I began to read and to pray.
-- My roots took hold.
                                        Her roots took hold!

Forward I went, slowly day by day.
-- My seed sprouted!
                                        Her seed sprouted!

For God's great love is food for my seed,
To give me strength to conquer sin and greed,
Jesus works through me, fulfills every need,
-- I grew branches!
                                        She grew branches!

I want to learn, God has opened my eyes.
I'm still not smart, He's the one that's wise.
I trust in Him to mold me into size.
My joy every day is a new surprise!
-- Jesus blessed me!
                                        Yes, He blessed her!

I grow as I learn. The Lord sets the pace.
-- I can see now!

                                                    She can see now!

I'm saved - not by deeds, but by God's own grace.
-- I am free now!
                                                    She is free now!

Life here on earth is a gift so rare,
There's no other way that can compare,
With God's great love which we all can share,
-- In forever!
                                                    Yes, forever!

What my life has become I compare to a tree.
My branches grow as God strengthens me.
And I have been changed for all to see.
I may even bear fruit by helping thee,
-- In the future!
                                                    Hallelujah!

Considering Salvation

Reflection

What have you accomplished in life, my friend?
Have you learned that earth's treasures will come to an end?
Have you left behind goodness, or left behind grief?
Can you drift off in slumber and sleep with relief?
Did you learn through the years many lessons in life,
Or are you resentful and bitter of strife?
Did you set an example of love and of trust,
Or live your own rules of cheating and lust?
Did you hoard and collect great material wealth,
Then share it with others, or keep it yourself?
Were you honest when working, good effort you made,
Or quite undeserving of what you got paid?
Did you think other people were equal to you,
Or point out their faults with a critical view?
Did you love your neighbour when their back was turned,
Or ridicule them, telling all what you've learned?
Can you look in a mirror and like what you see?
Then say to that person, "I'm glad to be me".
Did you learn what you've given is all you'll receive,
You'll be judged in Heaven, or don't you believe?

There's still time to change, a race yet to run.
When your heart stops beating, your chances are done.

Destination

So you don't want religion? You run your own show?
And you're in control of wherever you go?
You are your own boss and do what you want?
If I follow the Lord, you may even taunt?
The end of the world? Don't worry, my friend,
We're both going to die, however the end.

Great things have been promised, don't let yourself mope,
You choose only this life, but I have got hope.
Yes, hope for a future beyond this life's fears,
And unending peace without any tears.

This world is a classroom of lessons we need,
To overcome hate, pride, envy and greed.
To learn to forgive, and also, to love,
To prepare for our future in Heaven above.

If there's any chance that you're wrong and I'm right,
Just check out the Bible and follow the Light.

Too Late
(a dream)

When I was young my mommy worked,
I had to stay alone.
My dad had left and not come back,
And we were on our own.

Mom held two jobs to make ends meet
And she was always tired.
We sometimes had no food to eat
Whenever she got fired.

Mom said I made it hard for her,
When I asked her to stay home.
I told her I was scared at night,
While I was all alone.

She told me not to bother her,
Or something cruel like that.
"Go to your room!" "Leave me alone!"
"Quit acting like a brat!"

How come I feel frightened? Why am I always sad?
How can I be happy when I seem to make mom mad?
Why did you not tell me about God up above?
Why did you not tell me that God is full of love?
I only needed someone to listen to my fear.
All I needed was to know that God is always near.

I wanted to be like other kids,
I'd see them laugh and play,
Then ask mom just to play a game.
"Don't bother me," she'd say.

Mom told me I was just like dad,
Whining and afraid.
And if I'd gone with him, you know,
A good life she'd have made.

The kids around the neighbourhood
Would pick on me and fight.
I never won - I'd just run home
And cry all through the night.

I grew up without any friends,
The kids said we were poor.
They told me my mom worked all night,
Because she was a whore.

How come I feel frightened? Why am I always sad?
How can I be happy when I seem to make mom mad?
Why did you not tell me about God up above?
Why did you not tell me that God is full of love?
I only needed someone to listen to my fear.
All I needed was to know that God is always near.

I could have stood all this abuse,
Through fire I would have trod,
If just one person told me,
About a loving God.

I decided what I heard was right,
That I was a mistake.
So I swallowed forty sleeping pills,
My young life I did take.

Please think of what I'm telling you,
The effect of words you speak.
Material things aren't what kids need,
Your love is what they seek.
It isn't their fault they were born,
Don't blame them for your strife.
Hug them, build their self-esteem,
Give them a chance at life.

Tell them what you know of God,
And that He's always near.
Tell them God is full of love,
And help them with their fear.

This never should have happened,
I withered up - then died.
For my young life was wasted,
And all God's angels cried.

How come I feel frightened? Why am I always sad?
How can I be happy when I seem to make mom mad?
Why did you not tell me about God up above?
Why did you not tell me that God is full of love?
I only needed someone to listen to my fear.
All I needed was to know that God is always near.

All I needed was to know that God is always near.

The Verdict

Are you ready to stand before the mighty throne of God,
To be judged for what you did while here on earth?
Then find you stand alone, and must answer for yourself,
With no one else to validate your worth?

No excuse can pardon what God knows about your life,
The special gifts the Lord gave you to use.
God loves you and will guide and comfort you in every way,
But life is short, you have no time to lose.

We all are hoping that our life will be a lengthy one,
To live at least our four score years and ten.
But we don't have the power to speed or slow the hands of time.
God only knows our fate of where and when.

Life's Shelter

Some people are afraid to die,
And some afraid to live,
But you can overcome that fear,
If your heart to God you give.

You future life is guaranteed,
And present life is peace,
The Lord will lead you every day,
His love will never cease.

Premature

How was he to know that this night would never end,
That he'd wake up in a place where he didn't want to be,
Especially when he realized - it was for eternity.

He was only in his teens and oh, the plans he had!
He dreamed of living on his own away from mom and dad.
They tried to stifle him with rules, "You must live right, not wrong."
"Just be like us," they told him. "Stay where you belong!"

"No way," he thought. "How boring! There's lots I have to see.
Religion's just for old folks, not when you're young, like me!
My parents are so out-of-date and foolish in my view,
I'll show them what success is; what money and power can do!"

"I'll make a lot of money to buy great luxury,
A fancy car and lots of booze; the girls will flock to me!
We'll party through the daylight; we'll party through the night,
I'll be so happy mom and dad will see that I was right!"

How was he to know that this night would never end.
That he'd wake up in a place where he didn't want to be,
Especially when he realized - it was for eternity.

Change

On Being Brave

Sometimes we can't see what is happening until we have a chance to look back and reflect. This happened to me. For the last three years I'd been thinking about being baptized by immersion, but every time it took place at Elora Road Christian Fellowship last year there was some reason why I didn't step forward—I was sick, away, or just plain NOT BRAVE. But I think the Lord had a different plan and now I'll tell you the story.

Dave and I have been married for thirty-three years and we moved into the Belwood area eighteen years ago. I started attending the Belwood Church but Dave wasn't interested in going and the more I asked, the more he dug in his heels and refused. But I was very anxious for him to know God so I kept at it, inviting Dave to all the Church events and trying to get him to visit other Church members to no avail. Needless to say, my efforts were not working.

After years of reading and praying, God finally got through to me and I realized it was not up to me to bring my husband to the Lord. It was up to God in His own timing. In fact my actions could possibly be a stumbling block in Dave's path. So I backed off my good intentions and continued to worship alone. When I stepped away, the events started to unfold and it's glorious to look back and realize what God can do.

For twenty-three years we spent the winters camping here and there in Florida, but we had never stayed in a campground that held Church services. Two years ago we changed campgrounds and found out the owner was trying to get a Church started in the rec hall. He knew a young Baptist pastor who agreed to put on a service every Sunday.

When Dave and I arrived, I noticed a full-size electric piano covered with a cloth at the front of the rec hall. I don't read music but like to play old hymns, but couldn't figure out how to even turn this one on. So I asked two men sitting outside if either of them knew anything about the piano. One man stood up and said he did—he owned it and was also the owner of the campground. I played a couple of songs and he said I played just like his daddy used to.

The owner said about forty people attended church but they didn't have anyone to play the piano. He asked if I would play some good old southern Baptist songs.

Well, I am a Canadian and had never been to a southern Baptist service before,but—BE BRAVE—I said I would think about it. Sunday arrived and Dave said he would go with me to the Church service—WOW! So we went together and both liked the young pastor Daniel. We introduced ourselves and—BEING BRAVE—I said I could play the piano by ear and could play a couple of songs that I knew before the service started. He was delighted.

The following Sunday Dave said he would go with me and sit in the front row to give me some confidence. THANK YOU LORD, and every week we enjoyed pastor Daniel's sermons more and more. By February there were one hundred people coming to the service. The funny thing is that very few people were southern Baptists as all the winter people were seniors from the northern states and Canada and they knew the hymns I played.

This past winter I again played piano for the services. The pastor said he would like to hold a baptism by immersion in the swimming pool beside the rec hall. I told Dave I was going to be baptized but didn't ask Dave any questions. The following Sunday Dave told the pastor that he would also like to be baptized. HALLELUJAH – PRAISE THE LORD. The next Sunday during the service and feeling a nudge from God, I stood up and asked the pastor for the microphone—BE BRAVE. I told the congregation I had never been baptized except by sprinkling as an infant which was really my parent's choice. And even though I was already a senior, it was never too late. I loved Jesus as my Lord and Saviour—and now this was my choice so I was going to be baptized in the swimming pool. I never discussed it with Dave, just turned and handed him the mic.

Because we spoke of our commitment, five more seniors came forward and all seven of us were baptized in the swimming pool. The owner mentioned if we hadn't spoken, the other people said they would not have come forward. And that's why I think this was God's plan.

So be brave, step out, and follow what God is nudging you to do.

How in the World Did I Ever Quit Smoking

I started smoking cigarettes at fifteen years of age in 1961. My favorite uncle used to entertain me by blowing smoke rings and I was enthralled. My father smoked a pipe constantly unless he was in the barn, or Church, and most of the teenagers in our farming community also smoked cigarettes.

I was shy and lacked confidence; smoking cigarettes made me feel more like I fit in with my peers and smoking was accepted by almost everyone as the thing to do in the sixties.

My, how things have changed!

My girlfriend lived three farms away from ours and she and I would meet at the back of my father's farm where we hid a pack of cigarettes and a book of matches in a deserted groundhog hole at the base of a large tree. We would look furtively around to make sure no one was watching and then retrieve the cigarettes and each light one up. We would inhale the smoke, cough, laugh, cough, and get so dizzy we could hardly stand up. But we would persevere until our cigarettes were finished. We wanted to be able to smoke around our peers without coughing or turning green.

Eventually we each bought cigarettes and moved the packs closer to our homes until we finally carried them with us always. I thought smoking was relaxing and enjoyed the rush of confidence that nicotine gives, and wouldn't contemplate the thought of it possibly being addictive.

I smoked a pack of cigarettes a day - every day. I can remember trying hard and being determined to learn how to smoke properly; to hold the cigarette correctly between my fingers; to inhale and not cough when inhaling. And of course, how to blow smoke rings.

It took some years before little negative symptoms started creeping into my thoughts. I coughed more and if I caught a cold it lasted longer than it used to. The price of cigarettes started rising which made the cost of smoking more apparent. The skin between my fingers was becoming a bit stained from the nicotine in the burning cigarettes and my teeth weren't as white as they used to be. But I was now finished school and working so the income easily paid for cigarettes without any stress on my part. I was in a group of fun friends and we all smoked. Anyone that didn't was ostracized and we thought of them as "goody-goodys".

Occasionally we would hear negative remarks about the effect of smoking on health but I tried hard to ignore them. The years passed and in my thirties I started noticing that some friends had quit smoking. The price of cigarettes kept rising and a few times I added up the money spent on buying cigarettes. But I continued to smoke the same number. That was the daily requirement of nicotine I was used to and any change of routine would make me become stressed and irritable.

I was diagnosed with bronchitis; then eventually chronic bronchitis because a cold or the flu would keep me sick for weeks at a time. And my illnesses became habitual in the fall and winter of every year. My energy level was also less but I brushed that symptom off as becoming older of course. But the negative symptoms of smoking over such a long period of years were becoming more and more apparent. I decided to try and quit.

Cutting down the number of cigarettes smoked in a day only lasted a short while. One tense situation and I was back to a pack a day. Over the next few years I took a Smoke-enders course, tried hypnosis, cut down my volume numerous times, tried quitting "cold-turkey", replaced smoking by snacking or chewing gum to no avail. I tried to quit by being hypnotized, by wearing nicotine patches and another time wearing buttons on my ear-lobes to push when I felt the urge to smoke, but all attempts were in vain.

    I threw many packs of cigarettes out the window of my car while driving, then shortly going to a store to buy more, thinking it just wasn't the right time to quit. I just couldn't find anything that would make me stop smoking. Every failure made me lose more confidence in my ability to succeed.

    My addiction was increasingly obvious and also my poorer health, deeper voice and terrible cough. Now desperate and very unsure of ever succeeding, I finally had to accept the fact that I was truly addicted to nicotine and smoking cigarettes and couldn't quit alone. I needed God to help me break this addiction.

    My husband and I tried the program of using a prescription from our doctor to help stop smoking called Zyban but my husband was allergic to it and broke out in hives. I finished both prescriptions while continuing to smoke but felt a bit more confident in trying once more to quit completely.

    Then my husband had a serious surgery operation and promised his surgeon that he would quit smoking. His five day stay in the hospital was his quitting point and he never smoked again. When he returned home from the hospital a non-smoker, I was stunned for I had to support his efforts by not smoking in our house or around him.

    Then I got sick with a bad cold. I also ran out of cigarettes and just couldn't ask my husband who had so recently quit, to go into a store and buy cigarettes for me. I also felt God was finally getting my attention – that if I didn't quit smoking soon, my health would never recover. But I would have to quit eventually because some day I would be hospitalized with illnesses and smoking would be taken away from me. I was at a "do or die" crossroads and knew it.

From that moment of decision on, I asked God to help me never take another puff – not even one. And we did it – God and I. After thirty-eight years of smoking a pack a day, I managed to quit. The hardest thing I have ever accomplished in my life – but we did it! The most gratifying – we did it! The most confidence-building reward I've ever had. And now I feel able to do anything in God's plan for my life.

But I must never have another puff of a cigarette. For the saying is true, "You're a puff away from a pack a day". I'm addicted to nicotine for life.

But we did it! Praise God Forever. I'm a non-smoker.

The Stash

Up the steps of our aluminum stepladder I climbed until I could reach the brown square in the ceiling. I lifted and pushed aside the heavy wooden trap door leading into the attic. This area was the only extra space available in our tiny cottage. Through the small opening, we had lifted and shoved box after box of clothing, still in good shape but our waistlines had outgrown them.

It was silly but we clung to the belief that at some future point in time, after a specific combination of diet and exercise, these clothes would once again adorn our lithe bodies. What dreamers we were!

Near the boxes of clothes, we had also stored cases of empty preserving jars which had once lined the shelves in the pantry. My mouth watered as I pictured the jars full of peaches, pears, berries, pickles, and relishes which had helped feed our family during the long cold winter months. I had gardened most of my life and the contents of these jars had been the payoff which I'd preserved throughout September and October on the farm. Now our children were grown up, adults living with their own homes and gardens. These boxes of empty jars only attested to a past way of life that no longer existed for us.

Also stored in the attic were large green plastic bags knotted tightly at the top. Paper labels taped to their sides listed the contents. Towels and blankets which no longer matched our décor; sheets for twin beds we no longer owned; children's toys and yards of unused material; curtains and drapes which had hung on windows of past houses we no longer lived in.

Sitting on the floor, scanning the attic, memories flooded back from years gone by. But I realized, what useful purpose were these physical memories to me? It was time for these items to be cleaned and scrubbed so that they could make new memories for other people. There were still many folks in need of towels and clothing, old toys, twin bed sheets and preserving jars.

    I quietly apologized to God for my unintentional hoarding. With energy and purpose renewed, I began carrying the first of many boxes and bags back down the stepladder to donate to a new generation of people to make their own memories.

Christian Life

The Christian Farmer
An Ode to My Dad – Herbert Frederick Alton

My father was a farmer I can tell you all today,
He worked the land and milked the cows, grew crops and lots of hay.
He usually worked from dawn 'till dusk and always did his best,
But when it came to Sunday – that was dad's day of rest.

Some farmers in the neighborhood worked when the sky was blue,
And if it was on Sunday – that is what they still would do.
But dad would be in Church that day dressed in his suit and vest,
For when it came to Sunday, that was dad's day of rest.

We'd pass them on our way to Church, out bringing in their hay.
The angry clouds were rolling in, but dad was going to pray.
"The Lord will give me time," he'd say, "to get the haying done.
And sure enough, the following week, out would come the sun.
Dad lived all his working years a steward of God's earth,
For he was born a farmer right from his day of birth.
God would test him now and then with a warm and sunny day,
But dad would load us in the car and go off to Church to pray.

Now though I strayed for quite some time before I turned to Thee,
I'll always thank God for my dad, an anchor firm for me.
The lesson we can learn from this, God tells us that it's true,
Is not just taught by what you say but also what you do.

An Ode to My Mom – Margaret Grace Alton

Sometimes if I'm lonely and also feeling glum,
All I need to cheer me up is telephone you, Mom.

You've always been there for us, a rock we leaned upon.
You loved us from our day of birth, Charlie, me and John.

You turned your house into a home by welcoming everyone,
And when the holidays arrived, we sure had lots of fun.

You didn't smoke, you never swore, and wouldn't take a drink,
It didn't make me act the same, but certainly made me think.

At penmanship and keeping books, you really did excel.
And making pies and knitting were more gifts you did so well.

When playing bridge or euchre, better cards was your one wish,
But you were always lucky when it came to catching fish.

You've passed on many gifts to me – poetry was one,
Growing and preserving food and how a home is run.
And when grandchildren came along, you loved them just the same,
Helping in a thousand ways – now "Grandma" was your name.

You taught me to appreciate God's beauty everywhere,
All of nature's little things are treasures, oh so rare.

And so Mom, as this poem ends, I just want you to know,
You've touched a lot of people's lives and we all love you so.

Criticism

Please help me to realize
that I am not to criticize,
Another's point of view.

For I have faults that they can see,
which need correcting within me,
So that's what I should do.

For even if they're lacking, Lord,
So am I -- it's true.

I'll try to only change myself,
and leave them up to You.

Daybreak

Thank you Lord for giving me
A golden opportunity,
To honor You throughout this day
In all I do and what I say.

For yesterday is over now,
Tomorrow's not in view.
So guide me through the present time,
I give today to You.

Last Chance

Even though my mind's expanding,
While I live upon this earth,
There are situations I can't grasp,
Or understand their worth.

But some day I shall move beyond
Earth's chains with which I'm tied,
Then rise toward the heavenly plane,
With Angels as my guide.

And there the answers will be told,
My final outcome sealed.
The jigsaw puzzle finished,
And my part in it revealed.

So if I must correct mistakes,
The chance is only here.
I now try to achieve my best,
Each day throughout the year.

Truth

Don't categorize people,
By what they look or sound like,
We all are human beings with a creed.
Our worth is not just living,
It's learning to be giving,
To help another person who's in need.

Personal gain is empty,
To help someone – fulfilling,
To take advantage is a terrible wrong.
The earth has all the bounties,
That people could desire,
We only have to learn to get along.

Remember

God trusts you to be faithful, love all and do your best,
Then He'll reward you greatly, with eternal Life be blessed.

We're not in charge of deciding which actions succeed or fail,
But we should ask God's guidance, it's His plan that will prevail.

Don't listen to people's grumbling or heed their petty woes,
You qualify for the job at hand because it's you God chose.

But being lazy and idle, if careless life you choose,
Then fear and worry will prevail and everything you'll lose,

If God gave you a gift to use, you better get right to it,
Or you may find your chance is gone and someone else will do it.

Repose

How can I tell you life's hard, dear Lord when You have died for me?
How can I tell you it's hard, dear Lord to keep my eyes on Thee?
How can I tell you I often stray to the easier path that's not Your way,
Please help and guide me through this day, I yearn to follow Thee.

I fight within myself, oh Lord, to do what's right, not wrong.
Please turn me from ungodly thoughts and help me to be strong.
I want to be a light for You, to shine in all I say and do,
So help me please to work this through, to You Lord I belong.

As I pondered this with weary heart, a peace came over me,
And Jesus whispered in my thoughts, *"I can do all things through thee.*
Don't take the lead, for you are mine, just rest your weary head.
I've overcome the world you know, for you my blood was shed.

For I have put a new spirit in you and removed your heart of stone.
Replacing it with a heart of love, now you are my very own.
So follow God's laws and live for me, a shining light you sure will be,
For I have changed you for all to see, never more will you be alone.

*Just work each day and do your best, for I will be there too.
Give your burdens to me, dear one, and I will see you through.
Try to lift others up with love, I give you strength from God above,
For I am the hand within your glove and I will work through you."*

Through the Fog

One morning I arose and stepped outside. It was so foggy that I couldn't see any distance. All the landmarks had disappeared into the mist and I felt lost.

I started my daily prayers and realized that the Lord can see us clearly even if we can't. We sometimes get ourselves into situations where we are stumbling with indecision, like trying to find our way through the fog.

The Bible tells us that nothing can separate us from the love of God. If we focus and strive toward Jesus' teachings, we are on the right track and need not be afraid. We are never alone or isolated and can put our trust and confidence in Jesus to guide us safely.

My White-Haired Soul Sister

I lost my sister-in-law Joan to cancer. The cancer took her from a driving force of energy, fun, and enthusiasm to being bed-ridden before it took her life at age sixty-one.

The cancer took so much from her but it couldn't touch Joan's spirit, her love for Jesus, family, friends and people that radiated from her. The cancer couldn't touch Joan's soul. In fact, it made many of her Christian attributes stand out more and she taught me wonderful lessons about life and how we should live it. These are some of the things she taught me.

"Always be full of joy in the Lord. I say it again – Rejoice!" (Philippians 4:4 NLT).

Joan was always so thankful when saying grace. As we lived about thirty miles apart, Joan and I often met at different restaurants for lunch and a visit. I felt awkward saying grace out loud in public, so I usually asked Joan to say the blessing. Now Joan was a devout follower of Jesus and she was thankful for everything, always thrilled to have a chance to represent me and say grace in these restaurants.

With heads bowed and eyes closed, Joan would begin by thanking the Lord for the day; for the chance we had to share the meal together; for the joy she had being with me; for our families, our children, our grandchildren, our health, our ability to serve God. The food was starting to get cold. I was getting uncomfortable in this public place, knowing many people around our table were trying to keep quiet and be gracious and polite, to not interrupt with noise from their own conversations. At last my dear sister-in-law would started thanking God for our meal, the waitress, the food that would nourish our bodies so we could use the nutrition to better serve. Finally Joan said, "Amen," and grace was over.

I'm sure Joan didn't realize how much longer her grace was compared to other people. She was just truly thankful for everything.

Be confident and rest in the peace of God.

"Whatever you have learned or received or heard from me, or seen in me - put it into practice. And the God of peace will be with you." (Philippians 4:9. NIV)

Losing someone you love leaves an emptiness that is hard to fill. It is difficult to carry on, but God says He will never leave us or forsake us.

When Joan lost her beloved husband Joe, she drew closer to God, and in the days, months and years of her illness, she remained in prayer and at peace, resting in God's Spirit. She turned over what she couldn't deal with or handle to Jesus. It was an amazing thing to watch Joan living in such peace and so thankful for all the blessings God had given her when we knew what pain and suffering she was enduring month after month.

It was hard to understand how she had to deal with giving up the work she so enjoyed; then her car, and the ability to drive; from making her own meals to graciously accepting whatever other people made or brought for Joan to eat; her mobility of being completely independent to becoming completely dependent on others. And finally the effect on her body as the cancer slowly took its toll; having to move away from her own house into the homes of her children to take care of her; giving away all her possessions and selling her house which she personally designed and oversaw it's construction.

    That didn't bother Joan because she knew what we have on earth all belongs to the Lord. We are God's stewards in this lifetime. We leave the world with nothing material. But we do leave behind the example of how we lived while on earth which is passed on to the generations to follow.
Our treasures are in Heaven with Jesus. Joan was a shining example of love for Jesus for me to follow and she will always be my mentor.

With love from Sue

My Daily Boost

I need a little piece of God to help me start the day.
A passage from God's Bible to guide me on my way.

I've read from other authors, their little bits of news,
Or headlines in newspapers with mostly negative views.

But they don't keep me positive or give me strength to cope
With what this day's agenda brings, to encourage and to hope.

It's easy in this world of ours to get sidetracked by woe,
For war and crime and violence are everywhere we go.

But I believe in doing good and treating people fair.
To put their needs ahead of mine and let them know I care.

So I need a little piece of God to help me start the day.
A passage from Gods Book of Love to guide me on my way.

Our Worth

What use am I, oh Lord above?
What use am I to You?
You must be disappointed
In the things I say and do.

I'm just a bruised and broken shell
Of what You did intend.
And now I'm getting up in years,
New chances soon will end.

Sometimes I am so willful,
And don't do right - but wrong.
Temptation wins the battle,
I'm weak instead of strong.

"Oh child," God said, "you're precious!
I'll fill you full of love.
So you can face your trials each day
With guidance from above."

So I knelt down on bended knees,
Tears welled up in my eyes.
To give thanks to Almighty God
Who considered me a prize.

Then I made a list of blessings,
And gifts God gave to me,
That I could pass to others,
To help humanity.

We Are Never Alone

In the early morning, while still dark at my house, I watched an airplane traveling across the sky. The sun was shining on it making the airplane as a bright light.

Suddenly the light disappeared. I wondered what had happened and felt sad the light had been taken. Then I realized the airplane was still there. A cloud had blocked the rays of the sun and without the light, the airplane was invisible to my eye.

I thought about Jesus and the disciples. Jesus is the Light of the World and the disciples felt safe and were comforted by His presence. Then Jesus died on the cross and the disciples felt lost, afraid and alone.

When the disciples saw Jesus again in the upper room, they were overjoyed. Because of Jesus' life, death and resurrection, we know He is alive forever with us.

I couldn't see the airplane though it was still there. We can't see Jesus but we can be confident knowing Jesus is with us always.

Whisper a Little Louder Lord

Whisper a little louder Lord, the television's on,
I read the newspaper today, my optimism's gone,
The kids are arguing again, I seem to be a pawn,
So whisper a little louder Lord, the television's on.

The pace that we are living Lord, is hectic as You see,
With everything computerized, life's modernizing me.
The stores are open Sundays now, some work from dusk 'till dawn,
So whisper a little louder Lord, the television's on.

Modern things are supposed to make life easier for me,
Technology should give us time to have more time for Thee.
But life is so advanced now, I feel just like a fool,
So now I spend the extra time in going back to school.

So whisper a little louder Lord, the television's on,
I read the newspaper today, my optimism's gone,
The kids are arguing again, I seem to be a pawn,
So whisper a little louder Lord, the television's on.

www.ingramcontent.com/pod-product-compliance
Lightning Source LLC
Chambersburg PA
CBHW071118090426
42736CB00012B/1941